To Doreen & George

God bless you

God is always in control!

Never Give Up.

Above the Storm

Anita Pearce

Rom. 8:37-39

ANITA PEARCE
Above the Storm

Guardian
B O O K S

Belleville, Ontario, Canada

Above the Storm

Copyright © 2004, Anita Pearce

National Library of Canada Cataloguing in Publication

Pearce, Anita, 1954-
    Above the storm / Anita Pearce.

Includes bibliographical references.
ISBN 1-55306-732-0.--ISBN 1-55306-757-6 (LSI ed.)

    1. Christian life. I. Title.

BV4832.3.P42 2004   248.4   C2003-906913-3

For more information, please contact:

Inspiration Ministries
Box 44
Margo, SK SOA 2MO
www.inspirationministries.net

Guardian Books is an imprint of *Essence Publishing,* a Christian Book Publisher dedicated to furthering the work of Christ through the written word. For more information, contact: 20 Hanna Court, Belleville, Ontario, Canada K8P 5J2. Phone: 1-800-238-6376 • Fax: (613) 962-3055. E-mail: publishing@essence-group.com. Internet: www.essencegroup.com

To my mother, Margaret Pearce,
whom I respect and admire.
Your faithful love, your prayers, and example,
have profoundly influenced my life.
With pride and love I dedicate this book to you.
I love you.

Table of Contents

Acknowledgements

The writing of this book provides me with the opportunity to express my deepest gratitude to many friends for their encouragement and support.

The following individuals are deserving of special thanks.

The board of Inspiration Ministries: who held me accountable to this project. Their friendship, encouragement, and prayer support have been a tower of strength.

Darlene Kienle: who has been a precious friend and encourager. For many years she has been my close confidante. Her perception and advice have been invaluable.

To Leanne Simpson: my dedicated secretary who helped to choose and prepare material.

To Alice Dutcyvich: who worked hours assisting with the manuscript. Her expertise, advice, and enthusiasm for this project have been a great encouragement.

To John Lucas: who insisted it could be done, and who gave me the final impetus to go for it.

Introduction

A s I walked across the tarmac to board the airplane, the icy wind bit through my coat and attempted to take my breath away. The plane lifted off and the world below, left wrestling with the tempest, was hidden from my view by driving snow and pelting sleet. Bouncing on the crosswinds, we steadily gained altitude. Suddenly we burst through the clouds into blinding sunlight.

Life is full of challenges, conflicts, and crosswinds. Living in the turmoil of an ungodly society may leave us buffeted and discouraged. In spite of this, the power of the Lord's presence can lift us high on wings of faith; we can soar above the circumstances.

For many years I have travelled worldwide as an itinerant evangelist. On the pages of this book I will relate Scriptures, observations, adventures, and revelations that have touched my life and challenged me to live in Christ—above the storm.

Chapter One

GOD IS IN CONTROL

When storms of life overwhelm us, we can lift up our hearts with hope. There is a God in Heaven. The storm cannot stop the power of God. He is the Master over the tempest; the wind must obey His command. The startled disciples confessed in Matthew 8:27, *"...What manner of man is this, that even the winds and the sea obey him!"*

Gazing at the star-studded sky, I am reminded of David's words in Psalm 8:4, *"What is man that thou art mindful of him...."* Although we are tiny specks in His vast creation, God loves us and cares for us as individuals. The wonder of it all! From that perspective, my problems aren't so colossal!

Today is the tomorrow that you worried about yesterday.

Travelling through Paris alone, I had to change train stations to make proper connections. Now I was standing on a Paris street corner in front of one train station, with at least four streets in front of me. "You will find the other train station just around the corner," the ticket agent had said. I stood, searching for some clue. Which street? Which corner? To complicate matters, I was carrying about fifty kilos of baggage on a luggage carrier.

Unexpectedly, an elderly stranger approached me and, addressing me in French, asked where I wanted to go. When I told him the name of the train station, he replied simply, "Follow me." After a momentary hesitation, I set out after him down the street. When we turned the corner, I saw the train station. To my dismay, I also saw three long, steep flights of stairs between the station and me. How was I going to carry all this baggage down those stairs?

To my astonishment, this diminutive, elderly gentleman picked up the two heaviest bags and carried them all the way down. I quickly grabbed the rest and trotted after him. We loaded everything back on the luggage carrier and he guided me to the ticket counter. With a huge smile he shook my hand, then bent down and kissed it! He turned and, in a couple of seconds, vanished into the rush hour crowd.

I believe in angels, God's ministering spirits. On various occasions I have been sure they have protected and helped me. In this adventure, I am almost convinced I was seeing one in action. I'm not sure however, because I have no Scripture to prove that an angel would kiss the hand of the beneficiary.

In Mark 6:48, the Bible says that Jesus saw the disciples *"toiling in rowing"* against the storm before He came to them. Perhaps He will use the very circumstances that are troubling you, to come to you.

Don't run from change; embrace it.

The sky was filled with singing birds and summer sunshine. There was so much to do on this beautiful morning, including the needed trimming of the ornamental shrub. I sat with the clippers, snipping my way around the bottom of the tree, totally engrossed in my work and thoroughly enjoying a sense of accomplishment.

Slowly I became aware of a tingling sensation in my legs. I must have sat too long in one place. Then it spread. Suddenly, the realization hit me. I was sitting right smack in the middle of an ant pile! They were indignantly urging me to move off the top of their house. An army in full battle cry, they were marching all over me. Move I did, doing something like a jig, a pow-wow, and a break-dance all at once. For the next few minutes, I moved everything that could move!

How often we become self-centred and contented, setting out to accomplish our own plans. Gently, at least at first, but ever so effectively, the Lord uses His uniquely persuasive tools to direct us in His plan.

An old song says it something like this, "God doesn't make us go against our will; oh no, He just makes us willing to go!"

Joseph must have been often puzzled by the strange twists and turns of his experiences. Some would call it fate, and fold up in despair. Some would accuse the devil, declaring that he was manipulating and destroying. Others would say he had brought his troubles on himself. Joseph could certainly have blamed all his woes on his brothers, but, ultimately it was God who was in control, directing in the smallest details.

Often, we are tempted to blame, to run, or to despair. For the child of God, there is a higher way. God's plans are grander and greater than our imagination can conceive. In a short time, we will clearly see His ways are far superior to ours.

The cross you may carry does not outweigh the grace of God.

I usually drive my own vehicle when ministering in Canada. However, while travelling in other countries, I am dependent on the kindness of friends to drive me from place to place. I am so grateful for their assistance, as piles of luggage can be difficult to handle alone on trains and buses.

When one is used to being the driver, riding in the passenger seat can give a totally different perspective of the way the earth turns. Somehow all vehicles concerned seem to go faster and more or less out of control. There can be a great temptation to inform the driver of your opinions and perspective. Some drivers can greatly enhance one's prayer life!

It is not easy to surrender the steering wheel of our lives to Jesus. At least, we would like to offer some suggestions of how He should accomplish things. Sometimes circumstances look quite out of control and we don't see matters from the same perspective as He does. In reality, however, my greatest security is surrendering control to Him.

In the face of world turmoil and tragedy, our hearts struggle with unanswered questions. Querying God does not change His love for us, nor mean that we do not totally love and trust Him. This is similar to a young child questioning his father. The father may be unable to explain because of the child's limited capability to comprehend; however, the inquiring does not change the love of the father, or the trust of the child.

Jesus said to Peter in John 13:7, *"What I do thou knowest not now; but thou shalt know hereafter."* In His time, all of our questions will be answered.

Expect a miracle today!

God's plans are enormous. His ability to organize events to fulfill His promises is monumental. Of the thousands of details that had to be exactly in place for Jesus' birth, think of these few:

- *The emperor needed money, so demanded national taxation.*
- *Everyone had to register and pay.*
- *Tax registration was to be done in the town of family origin.*
- *Jesus' imminent birth had been announced and was due upon Mary and Joseph's arrival in Bethlehem.*

God inconvenienced the entire nation, putting them on the move to pay taxes in their province of origin, to bring Mary and Joseph to Bethlehem for Jesus' birth, exactly like the prophet Micah had said over seven hundred years before. I would have been complaining loudly about the tax hike, about the difficulties of travel, about the loss of pay-cheques and working days, and about the bad timing; not realizing that God was literally moving heaven and earth to fulfill His highest purposes.

The next time I am inconvenienced, I need to remember that His plans are significantly larger than mine. I serve a magnanimous God!

During autumn, we watch the leaves turn from green to gold. In the coolness of the evening we observe the rising of the harvest moon. Truly, the seasons declare: *"The earth is the LORD's, and the fulness thereof; the world, and they that dwell therein"* (Psalms 24:1).

Our God orchestrates all creation; He directs the symphony of the universe. He is bigger than any problem we have!

Victor Hugo said, "When you have accomplished all you can, lie down and go to sleep. God is awake."

Gently slipping out of the ski station, the cable car started its ascent up the mountain. The ski slopes below were deserted, and for a very practical reason. There was no snow! Here I was in Switzerland, surrounded by some of the most famous skiing slopes in the world and *no snow*. The unusually mild winter meant bare slopes. I can't ski, but had come to see the majestic peaks and savour some fresh mountain air.

Looking now at the bare rocks and patches of ice below, I saw a machine working. It was making snow! Just a speck in comparison to the immense mountain, it was sending out a spray of freshly-made ice crystals.

This observation was a perfect reminder of the futility of man's highest achievements. The machine was working feverishly at the cost of millions of dollars, to make a few yards of snow that would soon vanish into the mountain streams. At the command of our sovereign and omnipotent God, millions of tons of the white stuff could fall in a few minutes—enough to bury man, machine, and mountain. You know, we're really not so big and smart after all!

When the servants of Jarius came running with the bad news that his daughter had died, Jesus said to Jarius, *"Fear not, only believe."* Those words can bring us great courage. When bad news is screaming at us from all directions, *"Let the peace of God rule in your hearts"* (Colossians 3:15).

God writes with a pen that never blots;
He speaks with a tongue that never slips;
He works with a hand that never fails.[1]

One evening at a women's fellowship, I was enjoying a warm flow of the Lord's presence. In just a few minutes I was to begin speaking. I noticed an odour like burning rubber and heard an ominous cracking sound. Turning to look for the source, to my astonishment, I saw smoke curling out of my amplifier!

Quickly we unplugged the equipment and the burning stopped. As we opened the door to clear the smoke, my thought was, "Wouldn't this have been good for an illustrated sermon about the last judgment!" The promise of God is: *"All things work together for good to them that love God, to them who are the called according to His purpose"* (Romans 8:28).

The next day it was possible to strike an excellent deal on some long-needed sound equipment. Out of what seemed like an enormous problem came an ideal solution.

In Romans 8:31, the Bible says, *"…if God be for us, who can be against us?"* What great words of hope to know that, as we walk with our hearts open to Him, God is on our side! The love of God encircles and upholds us. He is not the enemy of those that love Him, but our Friend! In the struggles of life, it is comforting to know our Friend is more powerful than the enemy! What peace and joy to rest in Him.

About worry, Sarah Jewett said, "It isn't worthwhile to wear a day out before it has begun."

For born-again children of God, there is the assurance that all the details of our lives are in His hand. If we live, we live for His glory with purpose, peace and power. If we die, we know we have eternal hope. There is no reason for pointless worry. No matter what happens, we can't lose for winning.

I heard of a woman who took her place on the train. She fussed while trying to get her heavy bag up on the rack. Then she fretted about the sun in her eyes. She stewed because the seat was uncomfortable, until she got a cushion to sit on. Finally, she was irritated because she wanted her knitting out of the heavy bag that was up on the rack.

Soon the conductor called her destination. "Oh my goodness," she said, "If I'd known the trip was so short, I wouldn't have fussed so much!"

World events are marked with both horror and hope. As we approach the end of this age, there will be more cataclysmic happenings on earth as kingdoms clash in the heavenlies. But none of these events will take God by surprise! Soon He shall have the last word. May we stay close to Him, ready to walk with Him into eternity.

Christ is no security against the storms, but is a perfect security in them. He does not promise an easy passage; He does guarantee a safe landing.

Every street corner in Taiwan has some sort of Buddhist temple. Near any one of them, the air can be heavy with the smoke from incense candles. I was told that, besides the worship of ancestors, the people pay homage to over 3,000 gods. They pay little attention to the good gods, but spend their lives forever trying to appease the bad ones. What a vicious circle of hopelessness!

The missionary was taking me on a mini-tour of the local Buddhist temple. It took a few minutes for my eyes to adjust to the dimly-lit room. The smoke from the incense was thick and had the smell of being *bad for the health*. As I looked around the room, I was immediately impressed by the large number of idols sitting on tables, platforms, and other stands. There seemed to be nearly a hundred of them. Some were made of wood, while others were made of different kinds of metal. All of them had ugly faces; some wore terrifying grimaces.

The missionary pointed to a man carrying an idol under his arm. It was about a foot long. He set it near several others that were at the front of the room. I was told that he had brought his god to get *recharged*. Obviously, the owner felt that his god was losing some of its power. The wisest action he knew to perform was to bring it back to the temple, to absorb some more power!

I was astonished to see highly-educated, three-piece-suited men bowing to the floor in front of a block of wood or metal. They were praying to something made by human hands that could not hear or see. The prophet says in Isaiah 45:20, *"They have no knowledge that set up the wood of their graven image, and pray unto a god that cannot save."*

My own heart leaped with joy. I don't have to recharge my God! *"Jesus Christ the same yesterday, and to day, and for ever"* (Hebrews 13:8).

What the enemy means for evil and destruction,
can be turned to God's glory. In the fascinating story of
Esther, we can see how the Lord directs every detail to
bring deliverance to His people. Take courage.
God will accomplish His promises and His purposes.

God does not give us grace for our imagination——but for our experience.

There was a long line ahead of me as I sat waiting in my car at a border checkpoint to the United States. Having had difficult experiences in the past, I greatly disliked border crossings! So now while I was waiting, I occupied myself with worrying and chewing my fingernails. At last it was my turn. By now, after twenty minutes of anxiety, my hands were clammy, my stomach was in knots, my heart was pounding, and my voice was squeaky.

The stern-looking guard asked the customary questions about citizenship. Next he questioned why I wanted to visit the United States. When I told him I was clergy and had been invited to speak and sing in several Full Gospel churches, he looked at me sharply. After a long, thoughtful moment he said, "I will give you a test. If you pass this test I will let you across the border. If you fail this test, we will forbid you to enter."

Taking a deep breath, he requested, "Quote John 3:16." Well, I am happy to say, I passed the test with flying colours!

When we worry, 98% of the time it is about things that will never happen. Someone once said, "A good test of your memory is to try to remember what you worried most about yesterday." Some people have the philosophy, *"Why pray when I can worry!"*

In Nehemiah 8:10, the people are encouraged to rejoice in the Lord: *"...for the joy of the LORD is your strength."* As we fill our hearts and our mouths with gratitude and praises to the Lord, His promises become personal experiences. The deep joy we have in Christ gives added stamina in the middle of daily conflicts.

He, who is a slave to the compass, enjoys the freedom of the open sea. Let the Word of God be your compass; it will not guide you astray.[2]

It took a mighty effort, with much tugging, pushing, and grunting, but finally all my baggage was securely stowed between the seats on the train. It was only that morning, several cities away, my friends had waved good-bye. Now, alone, I had mastered this train change. It was no small accomplishment with five large and heavy pieces of luggage. I settled down in my seat, pulled out the newspaper, and prepared for another leg of the journey.

My attention was suddenly attracted to the train parked beside ours. The train began to move. But which train? Was it the one I was on or the other one? There was momentary disorientation. No, our train was still beside the same station post. We had not moved! I watched the other train depart, marvelling at the visual deception. I settled back to reading the news. A couple of minutes later I glanced out the window again. I felt a little dizzy. Now the train station was moving! I shook my head and grasped for reality. Train stations do not move. Logical reason prevailed. The rush of changing scenery soon proved it was my train that was moving.

I started thinking about that optical illusion. Often we compare our spiritual progress, or our circumstances, or even church growth, to what we perceive as other people's experiences. We can deceive ourselves and think that we are really going places, when all the time we are not the ones moving at all. At other times we may think we are not advancing, when really we are moving and the others are sitting still! It's easy to misinterpret all the action around us by comparing our progress to other people and their circumstances.

We must always go back to the reality of God's unchanging Word. Let His Word be the measure of our progress in our journey through life.

Chapter Two

ALLEGIANCES OF THE HEART

Everything that we receive from the Lord comes through repentance and faith. Obedience springs from yielding to His will. Our surrender to the will of God unlocks the door to His peace and victory. One of the greatest promises of God's Word is found in 1 John 1:9: *"If we confess our sins, he is faithful and just to forgive us our sins, and to cleanse us from all unrighteousness."*

Sometimes, when we fail to live up to our own
expectations, we feel deeply disappointed with ourselves.
It is easy to think that the Lord also gives up on us.
Philippians 1:6 offers great hope and courage:
*"Being confident of this very thing, that he which
hath begun a good work in you will perform it
until the day of Jesus Christ."*

*We view maturity and success as the lack
of struggle in life, rather than the process of
struggling well. This thinking leaves us
ill-equipped to cope with the reality of failure.*

The tabernacle for the main camp meeting services was a simple structure used only in the summer. The doors were frequently left open for natural air-conditioning. I set up my sound system and threw the half-empty equipment suitcase into a corner behind the platform. I didn't need to look in it for the rest of the week. On Sunday afternoon, preparing to pack up the equipment, I pulled it out again.

When I opened the suitcase, out jumped at least five fat field mice! From the safety of a bench ten feet away, I called for help. Three husky men came to my rescue. One of them gingerly lifted the lid again and out jumped two more mice. There wasn't room for us all on the bench! One brave soul, whose courage shall surely make him immortal, successfully opened the lid and pulled out a whole mouse nest! In just four days, those mice, intending to make a permanent home, had constructed a cosy nest among the leftover speaker cables. That suitcase needed a thorough washing!

Of mice and sin, I learned:
- *They both can move in and take over quickly.*
- *They both love darkness, and soft, weak fabric.*
- *They both will run from bright lights.*
- *They both leave a smelly, dirty mess.*
- *With quick work and strong cleanser, things can be fixed up!*

In unsuspecting moments, dark thoughts can set up lodging in our minds, building nests of our vain imaginings, chewing holes through our moral fabric. It is only the Blood of Jesus that can wash out the contamination and reconstruct the heart.

The prophet Jeremiah had been given the task of warning the nation of Judah about God's impending judgment. No one was listening! Anguish for his rebellious people caused Jeremiah to be known as *the weeping prophet.*

Exactly as with the people of Jeremiah's day, rebellion, greed, hate and selfishness surround us, bringing despair and destruction. Like Jeremiah, we need God's grace to be faithful with the unpopular message of repentance, and to renew our compassion to pray for God's mercy upon our troubled world. We desperately need His grace and mercy.

People reject light, not because of intellectual or philosophical reasons, but because light shows their sin, and they would justify themselves.
——A. W. Tozer

In front of a large temple was a bronze statue of a sitting Buddha. As I walked past, I noticed a young woman and her husband. Leading him by the hand, she took him close to the statue. I watched with astonishment as she reached out her hands and softly caressed the statue's head and shoulders. With expressions of devotion, she and her husband bowed before it. I noticed that the bronzed head was polished by the caresses of thousands or even millions of hands that had reached out to it before.

In most of the Asian countries, one cannot help but be amazed at the amount of idolatry. I was filled with sadness to watch them bowing before the deities carved from wood and stone.

As I thought about this however, I realized that they were probably more honest and spiritually awake than many North Americans. Stuffed with self-righteousness, we bow before the gods of materialism, ambition, and pride. It was Oswald Chambers who wrote, "Pride is the deification of self." We are too sophisticated to confess these as the gods we worship! Even Christians can be caught up in the materialistic web, and devote their time and energy to satisfy their own selfishness.

Ahab was an exceptionally wicked king in the northern kingdom of Israel. Time and again God sent prophets to direct and warn him. He saw the miraculous power of God manifested many times, often right in front of his eyes. But he would not turn from his idolatry and wickedness.

What more could God do to convince him? Nothing—like multitudes in our world, who have had every opportunity to put their trust in Christ, yet refuse Him. No one is as blind as one who is willingly blind.

Men occasionally stumble over the truth, but most pick themselves up and hurry off as if nothing had happened.
——Winston Churchill

In his book of historical research, *The Decline and Fall of the Roman Empire*, Edward Gibbon gives reasons for the deterioration and collapse of the city. We are able to summarize them in these points:

1. *There was a rapid increase in divorce, promoting the destruction of the home and family unit.*
2. *There were higher and higher taxes imposed, with the public money being spent to give free bread to the people.*
3. *There was a mad craze for pleasure, with sports becoming more exciting and brutal.*
4. *There was the building of gigantic armaments in preparation for war, while the real enemy was deterioration within the moral discipline of the nation.*
5. *There was the decay of religion and the fall from faith to formalism; religion no longer offered moral guidance for the people.*

It is no idle proverb: *History repeats itself.* It is shocking to see the outlined similarities being produced again in our nations today. May God have mercy upon us and cause us to repent of our selfishness, greed, and lukewarmness. As Dr. Billy Graham has said, "If God does not soon judge America, He will have to apologize to Sodom and Gomorrah."

According to Hebrews 11, faith has much more to do with our attitudes and responses in the face of testing, than with the material results. For example, Moses' faith empowered him not to claim the treasures of Egypt, but to walk away from them. Let us desire the strength of faith that remains surrendered to Christ no matter what the circumstances.

The highest reward for a person's toil is not what they get for it, but what they become by it.
—John Ruskin

One of the trials of travelling is handling baggage. Between the young lady who was accompanying me and I, we had to arrange over one hundred kilos of suitcases, bags, and a guitar. We were carrying clothing, equipment, cassettes and CDs needed for a five-month tour. Getting that luggage through train stations was no small feat! The elevators were either too small, impossible to find, or not going in the right direction. The escalators seemed to be out of service or too narrow. In at least one instance, after a mighty struggle to get everything downstairs, we discovered we were supposed to be upstairs—not to mention almost missing the right train because we were on the wrong platform!

Apostle Paul said in Colossians 3:2, *"Set your affection on things above, not on things on the earth."* On the journey through life, don't become encumbered with unnecessary baggage and *don't miss the right train!*

The people came to Jeremiah the prophet (Jeremiah 42) and demanded of him the Word of the Lord. They promised that no matter what the Lord said, they would diligently obey. After Jeremiah clearly told them not to go to Egypt (where they wanted to go) they turned against him, mistreating him, and rebelling against the Word of the Lord.

We haven't changed much these days. Often we ask for God's will, but are really hoping that He will change His mind and let us follow our own desires. Someone has said, "We don't have to pray about disobedience!" May the Lord help us to quickly and willingly obey God's Word and do what we know He has asked of us.

Anytime you find that truth is standing in your way, you can be certain you are headed in the wrong direction.

Eight lanes of speeding traffic were heading west on the main highway through Toronto. Sticking close to a centre lane and concentrating on not getting run down, I chatted with friends as we travelled together.

I was suddenly reminded of my destination by seeing the exit I was supposed to take as it passed by on my right. I had missed it! With the heavy traffic, but mostly because I was distracted by the conversation, I had missed the turn-off! There was nothing to do but carry on until I could get turned around at another exit.

Arriving at my friend's home much later than I had planned, I had to explain how I had missed noticing, for ten kilometres, signs reminding me of the approaching exit! Wishing I had more adequate excuses, I had to admit that it was basically because I had been distracted.

Often we may miss the direction, the refreshing, and the comfort of the Lord, simply because we have been distracted from Him. Then we have to go the long way around. We miss His signposts, which point us to the inside track. The Bible admonishes us to *look to Jesus*. Let Him be the central focus of your life.

In the first chapters of Genesis, we hear the Father heart of God as He implores Cain to reject the temptation to sin and come again with a right sacrifice. How wonderful to know our God is a personal God who is infinitely and lovingly interested in you and me. He is not the disinterested, abstract force promoted by eastern and new-age religions. He calls us from sin to follow righteousness for our own good, that we can know the wonder of relationship with Him.

A message on a bumper sticker read: Lord, walk beside me with Your arm on my shoulder and Your hand over my mouth.

The snow was falling heavily as I drove through the night. Some roads were closed, but I was determined to keep my appointment to minister at an early service the following morning at a Bible college.

Arriving in the town, I finally located the house where I was to stay. It was across from the double doors of the Bible college. No one would be home, but the door would be left unlocked for me. Climbing over the accumulated snow banks, I carried my suitcase into the house. While I was groping for the light, I could plainly hear a radio loudly announcing the 4:00 a.m. news. "Why would somebody leave a radio playing that loud?" I wondered. Assuming it was to keep out intruders, I slowly took off my boots and walked up the stairs to where my room was supposed to be. Before turning on the lights, however, I felt a little uneasy. That noisy radio! In the reflected light of the street, I checked one room, then another, then the third room. To my astonishment, someone was sleeping in the bed! I was in the wrong house!

I descended the stairs somewhat more rapidly than I had ascended! I took my bags and made a speedy exit back to my vehicle. Some time later, I discovered another set of double doors at the Bible college and finally, the right house.

Among friends the next day, to everyone's great amusement, I related my unusual adventure of the previous night. I learned that the elderly lady who lived in that house was quite deaf and probably had not heard a thing. Living in the small town and across from the Bible college, she probably felt quite safe—very sure that no one from there would ever try to break in!

The spiritual application of that episode is simple. Make sure you are at the right place before you go through the open door. To permit this to happen, I also think that the God I serve has a great sense of humour!

Psalm 139 is surely one of the most beautiful passages in Scripture. I have been especially blessed by verse 2: *"...Thou understandest my thought afar off."* Our omniscient Lord not only knows the secrets and intents of our hearts, but also understands the deepest cry, the sequence of our reasoning, and the motives behind our very thoughts. All of this, and He loves us still. What amazing grace!

We judge others by their actions.
We judge ourselves by our intentions.

The tall, muscular, young man was impressive. His shoulder-length hair was unkempt, his arms were covered in tattoos, and a sleeveless vest hung on his large frame. I eyed him as he sat at the back of the church, and drew conclusions from his appearance. "This is a biker," I thought, "one of those rough, hardened street fighters, maybe even an escaped murderer! The woman and untidy fellow beside him are probably accomplices in crimes committed or in the making. Maybe he is here to cause trouble in the service."

At the end of the message, when I gave the invitation for those who wanted prayer to come forward, I saw him lean over to his two friends, whispering and gesturing. Then all three came forward. When I stepped down to them, I was surprised to see tears in the eyes of the big guy. With great gentleness and quivering chin, he reached out to me, asking me to pray for his friends. I was astounded to discover a huge, soft heart under that rough exterior. Recently converted, he was now powerfully influencing others to come to Christ.

A fashionably-clothed, middle-aged woman, with fine jewellery and pleasant perfume, came also. She seemed so elegant and my assumption was, "This refined person seems to have everything under control in her life." How very wrong I was! Between sobs, she shared an agonizing story of heartbreak, failure, and hopelessness.

Often we are influenced by appearances, actions, and biases. We quickly prejudge, drawing conclusions that taint our responses to those whom we meet. May our prayer be, "Lord, help us to perceive the intrinsic value You see—the Holy Spirit at work in every human soul."

Chapter Three

ATTITUDE FOR ALTITUDE

The most troubling circumstances can become challenges of faith, depending on our attitudes toward them. If we face our problems with the mind-set of anger or despair, the task seems long and the results have limited reward. However, if we tackle the crises with courage and cheer, we find joy in the journey. Paul entreated the church in Colossians 3:23,24: *"And whatsoever ye do, do it heartily, as to the Lord, and not unto men; Knowing that of the Lord ye shall receive the reward of the inheritance...."*

Difficulties will always pass our way. I am realizing that the Lord is not as interested in the circumstances as He is in our reactions and attitudes to these circumstances. These are always within our power of choice. We are what we have chosen to be. May the Lord help us choose to respond to circumstances in ways that please Him.

Success is more attitude than aptitude.

The young man who had been enlisted to drive me to the next service, suddenly exclaimed, "I think the car is losing power!" As clouds of black smoke billowed out of the car, he pulled to the side of the British Motorway. Apparently, the motor had a blown head gasket and had a number of other ailments. Thankfully we were near an SOS phone.

Listening to the monotonous roar of the speeding traffic, we waited for over an hour for a tow truck. I tried to think of everything I could be thankful for in this situation! Safety and the telephone were at the top of the list. When the driver of the tow truck accepted my CAA card, which meant no cost for a thirty-mile tow job, my gratitude list lengthened considerably. A taxi driver took us from the garage to the train station. Perhaps wishing to do a favour to a visiting Canadian, he took us the long route (I'm pretty sure), driving us through the centre of the city. In spite of the mounting fare, I had to look on the bright side, knowing that I would probably never have another tour like that of this city. After very nearly missing the right train and skipping supper, I arrived just in time for the service. My thank-you list continued to grow.

A grateful attitude, freely expressed to God and others, can quickly replace bitterness, frustration, and self-pity with peace and joy. However, I am surely thankful that every day is not like that one!

The story is told of an old mule that fell into a dry well. The owner decided neither was worth saving and began to throw dirt into the well to fill it up and bury the mule. The mule, however, simply shook off and tramped down the dirt that was thrown in. After enough dirt was packed in the well, he was up high enough to jump out.

The lesson is this: When someone throws dirt at you, shake it off and use it to take a step higher. Soon, what you thought would destroy you, will be the means that brings you to a higher place and even sets you free.

Philippians 3:13,14 says, *"...this one thing I do, forgetting those things which are behind, and reaching forth unto those things which are before, I press toward the mark for the prize of the high calling of God in Christ Jesus."*

A pearl is the product of a conquered irritant.[3]

Most of the weeds in my garden can be destroyed, or at least severely hindered in growth, by a good root chop with a hoe. But where I live, in Saskatchewan, there is one weed that turns the hoe chop into an excuse to multiply. So tenacious is this weed that, even when cut up, every leaf, every rootlet, and every branch turns into a new plant! Surviving, even *thriving* in dry weather, it patiently waits for the first droplet of rain to put down more roots. Farmers and gardeners alike had cursed it—until a neighbour discovered it is an amazing healing herb. To everyone's astonishment, she has turned that obnoxious weed into a valuable health food supplement and is selling it at $40 for a few grams!

Talk about turning a curse into a conquest! Talk about turning adversity into advancement! She's turning frustration into a fortune! She can potentially make more money from that weed than her husband has made from years of carefully-cultivated crops! Whatever may be the biggest trial in your life now, look closer. There is potential in it for God's richest blessing.

It is recorded in 2 Chronicles 34:3: *"For in the eighth year of his reign, while he was yet young, [Josiah] began to seek after the God of David his father...."* Then in 34:8 we continue to read: *"Now in the eighteenth year of his reign, when he had purged the land, and the house, he sent ... to repair the house of the Lord his God."*

Josiah's grandfather was one of Judah's most evil kings. Josiah's father had been so wicked that he had been murdered. But out of the ashes of this disastrous heritage, he made clear choices to serve the Lord, who became his God.

Perhaps your past is tarnished with abuse, rejection, sin, or selfishness. Rather than remain trapped as a prisoner of your past, you can make positive choices, take responsibility, and become more than a conqueror in Christ. Jesus can become more than the God of others; He can become your God.

The race is not always to the swift, but to those who keep on running.

At a women's retreat, one of the activities provided was an hour of aerobics in the early morning. Being a courageous early bird, and confident of my excellent physical condition, I decided to participate. I had never exercised in an aerobics class before.

It was an hour of huffing and puffing, jogging, and turning myself upside down in unusual angles. The other *amazons* were discussing how invigorated they were. I felt like collapsing! Of course I wasn't about to let any of them know that what was refreshing to others left me feeling like a wet dishrag. For three days I was discovering muscles in places where I never knew they existed!

To be strengthened, muscles need exercise. In the same way, our faith needs exercise. Sometimes in trials that come our way, our faith is left battered and bruised. Take courage: God uses life's challenges to stretch our faith. Sometimes the stretching brings pain, but it will produce power as we continue to walk in His Word. He has promised to be with us all the time, all the way.

Goliath threatened the armies of Israel; they fled to their tents in terror. When the lad David inquired, the soldiers told him of the impossibility of overcoming the giant. Sometimes we also feel overwhelmed by the magnitude of the difficulties in our lives. However, as paraphrased from John Maxwell's book, *The Winning Attitude*, this biblical account illustrates two ways we can view the immensity of our problems: The army groaned, "He is so big we cannot defeat him," but David exclaimed, "He's so big, I can't miss!"

In the confrontation between the stream and the rock, the stream always wins, not through strength, but through persistence.

Modern technology, with its computers and instant communication systems, can be a powerful tool to help accomplish more work with less effort. Although my skills are rather basic, I have found computers to be a tremendous help—especially with correspondence. When they work, they are simply fantastic; when they do not, they can produce great frustration and high blood pressure in a very short time.

So it came to pass, that the day I landed in Europe for a four-month tour, my computer decided to quit working! Sometimes I wonder if they don't have minds of their own! I discovered in short order that I was lacking a number of spiritual characteristics, including patience, mercy, gentleness, and faith! Of course I survived, and apart from some personal inconvenience, including borrowing other people's computers, all turned out quite well. However, a number of interesting lessons were reinforced:

- *If we have Jesus, we have everything.*
- *This problem too shall pass.*
- *What will this matter a hundred years from now?*
- *Technology is a tool to reach an end, not the end in itself.*
- *Be sure to sell the computer before the warranty is up!*

Discouraging circumstances can easily distract us.
We must lift our hearts to see the larger picture.
This present problem will not last forever. As we renew
our minds and focus on the Lord, His refreshing courage
flows into our hearts. Psalm 27:13,14 says, *"I had fainted,
unless I had believed to see the goodness of the Lord in
the land of the living. Wait on the LORD: be of good
courage, and he shall strengthen thine heart: wait,
I say, on the LORD."*

*A bend in the road is not the end of the road —
unless you fail to make the turn.*

With the sensation that my stomach was sinking into my shoes, I realized that I was the last person standing beside the airport baggage carousel. Where was my suitcase? Slowly I walked over to the lost luggage counter, casting hopeful, or rather wishful, glances back at the still-turning carousel. I was not in a particularly spiritual mood as I filled out the forms describing the lost bag. Everything I thought I needed in order to live was in it. I was thousands of miles from home and expecting to go farther in the next few days.

After numerous phone calls, I was calmly told that my luggage had taken a side trip—a thousand miles in the opposite direction! Carefully I took stock of all the earthly possessions I had in my handbag. It was suddenly not so bad. I still had my Bible, my passport, my comb, and toothbrush. As long as I had those things, I could survive anywhere!

Several days later, when my suitcase finally found me, my joy was subdued. Material possessions are handy to use, but ultimately, if we have Jesus, we have everything we need for time and eternity.

In 2 Chronicles 20:21,22, we read how the Lord gave a great victory to King Jehosophat and Israel. When it seemed like a hopeless battle, in obedience to the word from the Lord, they began to praise Him. Let us also lift up our hearts in praise to the Lord and watch the mountains of discouragement melt into molehills.

*Goals are like stars:
they are always there.
Adversity is like the clouds:
which are temporary and will move on.*

Keep your eyes on the stars.

The would-be thief was creeping gingerly along the power cable that was strung between poles, along the tree-lined roadside. With his four paws gripping the wire and his fluffy tail twitching nervously, the squirrel crept toward a bird's nest in the nearby tree. Then it happened! Two angry blackbirds, screeching their wrath, swooped down at him. Trapping him on the wire, they mercilessly pecked him and battered him with their wings. It was an intense moment—as good as any thriller, as they nearly knocked him from the cable. He turned tail and scurried away, giving up his dinner to save his life.

Several lessons were learned from that drama. The birds were small, their enemy much larger, but alertness had given them warning; righteous indignation gave them motivation; teamwork multiplied effectiveness; strategic attack gave them advantage.

The Bible declares that we also are in an ongoing warfare against the thief who wants to steal, kill, and destroy (John 10:10). Alertness to the enemy's tricks, motivation for righteousness, earnest battle in prayer, and unity with fellow believers can dislodge even the most persistent, obnoxious satanic forces.

In reading the book of Deuteronomy, I was impressed by how many times Moses used words similar to this: *"Beware lest thou forget the Lord."* Often, when everything is going well, we become self-sufficient and even apathetic in our relationship with the Lord. As soon as we have problems, however, we cry with great earnestness for the mercy of the Lord! Is it any wonder that He allows difficulties to cross our path, to remind us that without Him, we are nothing? May we daily live in the consciousness of His presence and never forget the faithfulness and mercy of the Lord.

Psalm 103:2 encourages us, "Bless the LORD, O my soul, and forget not all his benefits."

No nation on the planet, I am sure, has the ability to prepare and serve a meal with as much finesse as the French. One of the honours for visitors (*and sometimes the suffering*), is the famous seven-course meal. For a Canadian who can stuff down a whole dinner in fifteen minutes, French cuisine, demanding four *full* hours of table time, can be a challenge.

Gorgeous entrées, beautifully-arranged salads that should be on display in art museums, dozens of cheeses with unpronounceable names, and main courses cooked to perfection, are meals to remember! One could be killed with kindness!

I quickly discovered however, that when one is not hungry, after course number three or four, even the most delicious food loses its attraction. For the sake of good health, sooner or later exercise becomes imperative; if not walking, then at least rolling!

Could that be the problem with many Christians? We have eaten so well, and not necessarily what is most spiritually nourishing, that we have lost our hunger for God. Besides, we have done so little, it is with difficulty we follow Christ.

Life is full of enriching experiences. I have been
enthralled with the pageantry and excitement of young
friends' wedding celebrations. Looking at the perfection
of a friend's newborn baby filled me with awe. As I stood
by the bedside of an aged friend on the brink of eternity,
I was reminded of the brevity of our time on earth.
Daily I see the vibrancy, the wonder, and the frailty of life.

These observances have challenged me to be grateful.
I am *grateful* to God for His hope and peace, *grateful*
for friends, *grateful* for family, and *grateful* for life.

*Contentment is not found in having everything,
but being satisfied with everything you have.*

I had just finished a very encouraging week of services in Estonia. In spite of meagre salaries, short food supplies, and cold homes, the people had filled the church every night, their warm hearts glowing with worship. Now it was time for me to depart.

A lady about seventy years old, frail and bent, came toward me. Her coat was shabby and smelled of coal smoke. She was obviously one of those individuals living on a very small pension. Catching my arm, she chattered excitedly to my interpreter. There was a sparkle in her eyes and she was smiling happily. She pressed a package into my hands, then disappeared into the crowd. My interpreter told me it was a Christmas present and an appreciation gift for the services. Her granddaughter had prayed to accept the Lord during the week. I looked at the package. It was awkwardly wrapped in well-used Christmas paper. As I rolled back the paper, there was a jar of homemade raspberry jam.

Over the years, many friends and believers have graciously given gifts to this ministry and me. Given from hearts of concern and friendship, each gift has been greatly appreciated. Children have drawn pictures; some friends have offered souvenirs, and hospitality. Financial gifts have kept this ministry operating debt-free.

How can I explain what I felt as I held that jar of jam? I felt so small, so unworthy to receive from this woman. She had undoubtedly picked those raspberries from her meagre patch, storing them for her food during the cold winter months. Her need and poverty had not hindered her in this unselfish act of sharing. She had given the very best she had, the little bit of luxury that she knew, her sweetest dessert. At the same time, I felt incredibly rich to have seen such purity of motive and sacrificial giving. More clearly than ever, I understood what Jesus meant when He watched the rich giving their offerings. They were pious, but when the little widow gave her two pennies, she gave all.

I understand now that she and my elderly friend knew something that very few comprehend in the satiated societies of the west. Oh yes we give—and sometimes from our need, sacrificially. But this was far beyond. We only stand in astonishment at what they know: the joy of giving all in unselfish love.

When we are tempted to be frustrated and discouraged by the attitudes and actions of others, Hebrews 12:3 reminds us of the patience of Jesus and His response to the terrible things that sinful men did to Him. Christ's example gives us renewed courage and strengthened purpose in the face of opposition.

It is not what happens to us, but our response to what happens to us that hurts us the most.

——S. Covey

The thermometer registered -36° C, as I set out to drive my friend home. The gravel side road was partially covered with snow. Suddenly, I saw a porcupine waddling right down the middle of the road! Neither of us could escape the inevitable connection! With a bang and a bump it was over, and the rest of the journey was filled with pity for the helpless critter.

When we arrived at our destination, however, and I inspected the damage, all pity for the creature was forgotten in the wave of pity for me, and my van! The impact had completely shattered the frozen fiberglass bumper, the wheel well, plus who knew what else underneath. That plump little porky caused nearly $1,400 damage! I was astonished and very glad indeed that it had not been a moose! It was a relief to know that animal coverage insurance meant there would be no cost to me, and the inconvenience was minimal.

Seemingly insignificant happenings can do enormous damage very quickly. A careless word, an ungrateful act, a bitter thought, or a small offence can produce huge and painful results—some leaving irreparable scars.

David and his men fought and delivered the city of Keilah from the Philistine enemies that were about to destroy it in 1 Samuel 23. Shortly afterward, the Bible says that the people from the same city were very willing to deliver David into the hand of Saul to be killed. How could they be so ungrateful, cruel, and fickle towards David after he had hazarded his life for them? I am amazed at the merciful attitude that David was able to maintain toward them. May the Lord help us to extend graciousness and mercy to those who betray us.

Relationships don't thrive because the guilty are punished, but because the innocent are merciful.
— Max Lucado

There was still a certain heaviness that hung in the air as my friend and I walked through the gates of the concentration camp near Antwerp, in Belgium. Although many years have passed since prisoners were held there in World War II, and restoration provided for the comforts of tourism, the place was saturated with memories of horrendous suffering.

We walked through the dark hallways, peering through iron grates into clammy, cold cells. We inspected instruments of torture and envisioned human bodies reduced to skeletons by malnourishment and forced labour. I could not fully comprehend how human beings could be so cruel to one another.

On one side, we can see the cravings of pride and the lust for power, that debases men to become lower than animals, and results in incredible brutality. On the other side, in those who suffered and gave themselves to bitterness and hate, we can see the tragedy of slaves welding their own chains. Whether driven by pride or hate, it becomes a case of slave dragging slave, to hell, down the road of selfishness and self-gratification.

There is another way: the way Jesus taught—of love, forgiveness and surrender to Him. When we acknowledge our wicked, sinful hearts, recognizing that we deserve God's judgment for our selfish ways, we call to Him for mercy and forgiveness. Only then we can walk the new path to true liberty and peace.

The Bible is a spiritual book that is able to touch the deepest corners of the human soul and provide solutions to spiritual need. It is also a very practical handbook, providing principles for daily living. The book of Proverbs contains timeless wisdom that needs to be applied to daily circumstances. The key of wisdom is the fear of the Lord. From that reverence, we learn discipline of our attitudes, our tongues, our finances, and moral behavior.

The Bible is God in print.[4]

What challenge in the testimony given in Daniel 1:8: *"But Daniel purposed in his heart that he would not defile himself..."* Having seen the slaughter of his family, and now being held captive in a foreign land, this seventeen-year-old lad made profound choices to serve the Lord, at the risk of his own life.

We are responsible for the result of our own choices. Circumstances, people, and possessions may influence our decisions. Ultimately our attitude and character are created deep within, by our own choice. We are what we have chosen to be.

An unknown author penned these words:

You will never be sorry
For thinking before acting
For hearing before judging
For forgiving your enemies
For helping a fallen brother
For being honest in business
For standing by your principles
For stopping your ears to gossip
For bridling a slanderous tongue
For harbouring only pure thoughts
For sympathizing with the afflicted
For being courteous to all.

Chapter Four

DESIGNED WITH A DESTINY

The splendour of the universe displays the grandeur of God's imagination. Not only in its majesty and immensity, however, but also in the minutest details, we see pattern and design. Every person has been created to know Him and to love Him. In Philippians 3:10, Apostle Paul suggested that nothing was more precious to him than to *"... know him, and the power of his resurrection, and the fellowship of his sufferings, being made conformable unto his death."*

Although the children of Israel were liberated from Egypt and no longer slaves, they were never really free until they entered the Promised Land. That is because freedom is about responsibility. As long as they were slaves, and travelling in the wilderness, they were being managed. They were told everything they must do. When they entered the Promised Land they had to make decisions for themselves.

Many people refuse to take responsibility and to manage their lives after God's pattern, preferring to let circumstances and emotions dictate their actions. Responsibility, by contrast, will manage emotions and circumstances, to produce stability and spiritual success.

Some people dream of success, while others wake up and work hard at it.

It is not often that I have the opportunity to putter in the garden, but every spring my farmer's soul yearns to dig in the soil. Pictures in horticultural magazines of immaculate, bursting gardens deceptively lure one to dream of bulging baskets of vegetables and flowers. Somehow my beds of delicate flowers never end up looking like the books promise, but it's a pleasant dream!

Of course the first thing to be done in the spring is to work the soil. It has become hard. How is that possible? It was worked last autumn. There are at least four conditions that make soil hard: constant traffic, drought, frost, and neglect.

These are the same requisites that can make our hearts resistant: the constant traffic of busyness, with no time for the Lord to dig deep within; the drought of too many days without the rain of His refreshing; and the frost of bitterness and unforgiveness that freezes the soul. Finally, there is the neglect of weeks without His Word or prayer.

The prophet Hosea admonishes us in Hosea 10:12:

"Plant the good seeds of righteousness, and you will reap a crop of my love; plough the hard ground of your hearts, for now is the time to seek the Lord, that he may come and shower salvation upon you" (TLB).

Much of our discontent comes from focusing either on the blessings or curses of the future or the past. We often waste precious time wishing for the future or regretting the past. When we can learn to live in the *now*, and appreciate the benefits of each moment, our hearts can find sufficient grace. It is amazing how full our life can be when we draw out of each moment the abundance of the life God has given us. Let's *live life* now!

Live each day to the fullest; get the most from each hour, each day, and each age of your life. Then you can look forward with confidence and back without regret. Be yourself—but be your best self.

For the first time in many years, I was home with my mother at the right time to help with planting a garden. What fun it was to dig in the soft, prepared earth, and put the seeds into the ground. With my mother's *green-thumb* guidance I re-learned the art of making straight rows, planting seeds at the right depth, soaking peas for speedy growth, and cutting potatoes. We needed fertilizer and insect powder. We picked the stones that might hinder the growth of the tender plants and then turned on the watering hose. Everything grew great, including the weeds!

Our hearts are like a garden. The Holy Spirit, with His conviction, prepares our heart to receive seeds of faith from the Word of God. Gently He works to remove the stones of bitterness that would keep the seeds of love and kindness from growing. He reminds us to diligently dig out the weeds of cares and pleasures. He sends messengers across our path to water the Word with encouragement and exhortation.

How it must please Him to see the garden of our heart flourishing and bringing forth the fruit of *love, joy, peace, longsuffering, gentleness, goodness, faith, meekness, and temperance* (Galatians 5:23,24). On the other hand, what a tragedy it must be for Him to see our hearts overgrown with weeds of care, filled with stones of bitterness, hardened by selfishness and pride.

I could hardly wait to taste the fresh garden peas and carrots. Nothing can compare to the flavour of new potatoes, boiled, then served smothered in butter! We have the anticipation of enjoying the harvest. What bitter disappointment if it produced nothing!

The day is coming when we shall present the fruit from the garden of our hearts before the Lord. Shall we rejoice as we share the harvest with Him—or shall we be ashamed and empty-handed?

Jesus said in Matthew 6:28-30, *"And why take ye thought for raiment? Consider the lilies of the field, how they grow; they toil not, neither do they spin: And yet I say unto you, That even Solomon in all his glory was not arrayed like one of these. Wherefore, if God so clothe the grass of the field, which to day is, and to morrow is cast into the oven, shall he not much more clothe you, O ye of little faith?"*

The delicate beauty of forest and field reveals the majesty of God. Nothing in His creation is beyond the power of His care.

This evening, and every evening, turn your worries over to God—He's going to be up all night anyway.

It's so exciting to see the world come alive again in the spring and summer, after the long, dark winter. The air is filled with the aroma of flowers; the birds are busily raising their families.

I noticed some wild flowers growing in the ditch beside the road. As the world sped by, these flowers quietly spread their aroma, filling their corner of creation with beauty and praise to the Lord. The Lord could look at what His hand had made and find glory in the faithfulness of these humble, delicate blossoms. With petals reaching up in worship, not seeking acclaim, they were just doing what God created them to do.

No matter how large or small a flower may be, or how much it is recognized or ignored, or where it is located; within its being is the urgency to produce fruit. As long as it has life (and some species have a very short season), every ounce of its energy is joyfully involved to accomplish its purpose. The concern is not who notices or compliments it, but its desire to bloom and produce to the very best of its ability—often under great adversity or neglect.

How much more should we, as followers of the Lord, seek with all our might to please Him and present Him with an abundant harvest. Let's bloom where we're planted!

I held the little maple seed in my hand. So small and light, the wind had carried it to my doorstep. In that little seed was all the potential, not only of a full-grown tree but also of a whole forest. In some of the most insignificant details may be hidden the greatest solutions.

The message of a fridge magnet read, "All the flowers of all the tomorrows are in the seeds of today."

There is a law that has been established by God: *we shall reap what we have sown* (Galatians 6:7,8). What we sow will come back to us:

- *If we sow mercy, we will obtain mercy* (Matt. 5:7).
- *If we sow forgiveness, we will obtain pardon* (Matt. 6:14).
- *If we sow tears of compassion, we will obtain sheaves of souls* (Ps. 126:6).

The Word of God also makes it crystal clear that if we sow to the sin and flesh, we'll reap death and corruption. If we sow hatred and strife, we will be caught in that same trap.

God is an excellent account keeper. If I want to harvest the blessings of God spiritually, emotionally, and materially, then I need to sow good seeds, and lots of them! I believe that even in eternity, I will reap the glorious benefits of well-planted words and attitudes. Someone advised, "Keep your words sweet; you may have to eat them."

The gospel message at any time is only one generation away from extinction. If we neglect to plant the seeds of the gospel, or if we lose the seeds, there will be no flowers tomorrow!

When Jesus spoke the beatitudes, He was leaving His disciples instructions on how His followers should live. He was teaching them to show the world the love and character of God. He commanded them, and us, in Matthew 5:16: *"Let your light so shine before men, that they may see your good works, and glorify your Father which is in heaven."*

If you think you're too small to have an impact, try going to bed with a mosquito in the room.
——Anita Roddick

The Lord has brought many precious friends across my way as I have travelled along life's path. One of the people that marked my heart in a very special way was an elderly gentleman. Faithfully every month, for nineteen years, he wrote a charming letter of encouragement. Many times the inspiration of this gentle brother made a difference that only eternity will reveal. After a brief illness he went to his Eternal Home. I miss his cheerful letters, but am thankful and honoured for the privilege of having been his friend.

Often, we may feel insignificant or on the backstage of life. Like the young lad who brought his lunch to Jesus in John 6, what we have to offer the Master may seem so feeble, our resources so limited, and our talents so worthless. When we surrender them into the Lord's hand, however, and watch Him bless and break them into His design, we stand dumbfounded, beholding the masses He touches with pieces of our lives.

God is preparing His Church. We all have our place to fill. Some may seem more prominent than others, but all are important. We need to do all that we can do, as best as we can for His glory and for the edification of His Church.

Ephesians 2:21,22 tells how the Lord is building us: *"In whom all the building fitly framed together groweth unto an holy temple in the Lord: In whom ye also are builded together for an habitation of God through the Spirit."*

Many of us are the kind of do-it-yourself people who hit the nail right on the thumb.

Feeling rather ambitious during some of those rare days while I was at home, I did a little carpentry work. I built a table, some bookshelves, cupboards, and other pieces of office furniture. The drawers in the cupboards actually open and close!

To build something, a person has to have a pattern in mind first. Then the wood must be prepared by sawing and sanding. All the pieces need to be fitted together before it is nailed or glued. Every board and nail must fit in its place. Different nails are necessary in different places.

In my case, this fitting process could mean several more trips past the saw. Sometimes I'm like a carpenter friend of mine who told me he had cut the same board three times and it was still too short!

There are the finishing touches to do. The wood must be stained or varnished, and polished. Then comes the moment to step back and admire the accomplishment.

Jesus was a carpenter too. He is the maker of men who will submit to His hand. The Lord, in His faithfulness, has a great plan for each person. All through life, He saws and sands. Sometimes we do not like the sharp nails that pierce our being, but we know that He is making the final product to bring praise and glory to Himself.

There are *self-made* men.

There are *home-made* men.

There are *man-made* men.

Then, there are *Master-made* men.

What kind of man are you?

Chapter Five

HOPE IN THE DARKNESS

The clammy clutch of anxiety can paralyse the mind and cripple the soul. God's presence brings hope; His assurance lifts the heart. We carry on and find sufficient grace in Him. When addressing the church at Rome, Paul affirmed in Romans 5:5:

> *"...we are able to hold our heads high no matter what happens and know that all is well, for we know how dearly God loves us, and we feel this warm love everywhere within us because God has given us the Holy Spirit to fill our hearts with his love"* (TLB).

In the middle of Jeremiah's lamentations for the calamities that were happening to Israel, he drops this wonderful verse: *"It is of the Lord's mercies that we are not consumed, because His compassions fail not. They are new every morning: great is thy faithfulness"* (Lamentations 3:22,23).

Disasters daily disrupt the drudgery of our lives. Unforeseen circumstances can create crises in moments. Yet our minds can be filled with the peace of God's promises. His love is steadfast, even in the midst of conflict.

All the significant battles of life are waged within one's self.

The wind was blowing strongly as I stood on the summit of the hill overlooking the town of Vimy in the north of France. A spectacular view of the region could be seen from this height. Beside me on the ridge stood two immense columns of cement, built as memorials for the hundreds of Canadians who died gaining and holding this patch of ground during World War I.

In one of the many cemeteries nearby, I looked at the rows of grave markers and read the ages of some of those who had died. So many young men had given their lives in those battles. C.S. Lewis wrote, "War does not increase death." In every generation, death is total. Eighty-five years after the events of those battles, there are very few veterans still alive. Life is uncertain; death is sure. It is a wise man that recognizes the value of preparing for eternity.

President W. Wilson had declared, in 1918, that World War I would be a "war to end all wars." Yet since that armistice, the world has known even greater conflicts of genocide and holocaust. In our civilized world, hundreds die in war daily. Men simply do not have the ability to produce peace. The more people go around shouting, "Peace," the more war they make. How futile their efforts to make world peace while they have war in their own hearts.

The Bible makes the answer so clear. When we have peace with God, then we can have peace with ourselves. When that war inside is stopped, it is not difficult to have peace with others.

The twenty-third Psalm is perhaps one of the most beloved songs of David. The first verse is a summary of the confidence and hope that the Lord brings:
"The LORD is my shepherd; I shall not want."
In the busyness of life, whether at work or play, our spirits should continually be focused on our Shepherd. He knows what we need, and will walk with us through the times of difficulties, as well as the times of blessings.

If you can't sleep, don't count sheep;
talk to the Shepherd.

The road disappeared behind the curtain of blowing snow. Patches of visible road showed slick ice. There had already been a tragic bus accident on this highway a couple of hours before. It was -30° C in a roaring blizzard with eighty km/hr winds. I had a three-hour drive to get to the scheduled service that night!

This was one of those real northern Canadian winter storms! It was slow going. There were moments when I had visions of sitting in a snow bank, burning candles to keep from freezing, or of sliding in the ditch into the oblivion of that swirling snow. After three hours of wild imagining, fretting, fearing, and a good deal of earnest praying, I arrived safely.

Later, recalling the blessings of the service while tucked snugly into a warm bed in a country home, I was drawn to look out at the stars. The storm was gone and the stars were bright. It seemed I could just reach out and pluck them out of the frosty night sky. Suddenly, it was real to me once more: God knew where I was!

It is amazing how one can read a passage of Scripture many times, and then suddenly it comes alive in your heart. That is what happened as I read 1 John 4:9,10: *"In this was manifested the love of God toward us, because that God sent his only begotten Son into the world, that we might live through him. Herein is love, not that we loved God, but that he loved us, and sent his Son to be the propitiation for our sins."*

The message of the gospel is so simple, so wonderful. It is God's plan of redemption, reconciliation and relationship.

*God loves us just the way we are,
but He loves us too much to leave us that way.*
——Leighton Ford

While in Uganda during a two-week seminar, I was asked to preach the funeral service of a baby boy. He was scarcely a year old, the son of a national pastor. The casket was so tiny. The grave had been dug in a banana grove behind the pastor's home. I looked at the sorrow-lined faces. In spite of the pain, Christ gave them hope.

For those without Jesus, there is no hope. Death is just another cruel event in the vicious world. I had heard of Idi Amin's reign of terror. There had been sad whispers about the Loweto Triangle a few miles west of Kampala. It had become a place of mass graves, of piles of skulls, and unknown bodies left by the war.

What a difference there is for those who know Jesus! Death is merely the door of our hope, the total fulfilment of the peace and joy we already know. Paul, in 1 Thessalonians 4:13, admonishes us: *"...that ye sorrow not, even as others which have no hope."* Christ's atonement on the cross provides our eternal hope!

The deadly terrorist attacks on the World Trade Center on September 11, 2001, deeply shook our complacent society. In just a few minutes, buildings and investments, that many thought secure, were completely destroyed. Enjoying great freedom and wealth, we easily forget that outside of Christ, there is no security. James 4:14 says to us, *"...ye know not what shall be on the morrow. For what is your life? It is even a vapour, that appeareth for a little time, and then vanisheth away."*

Keep your focus on Jesus and remember: *Only one life, 'twill soon be past, only what's done for Christ will last.*

*This life is God's gift to us.
What we do with this life is our gift to God.*

Time waits for no man—and very few women either. Ever so often (and more often as time goes by), I am reminded of the fact that I'm not as young as I used to be. For example, I received a Christmas card from my fourteen-year-old friend that read, "You're the coolest old lady I know"!

On another occasion a supermarket checkout girl asked to see my senior's card! When I looked shocked, she added that, being only nineteen, everyone looked old to her. Then she continued, "I have a friend who is about your age, and she looks really old too"!

Is it vanity, pride, or simply trying to hide the secret of our wisdom, that in midlife we endeavour to keep from showing or telling our age? Is it the sudden awareness that life is passing too quickly?

When Dr. Billy Graham was asked what was the greatest surprise of his life, he replied, "Its brevity." We must live in the consciousness of eternity. In these troubled days, let us live each moment with the purposes of Christ as the priority of our hearts.

Light is amazing. In itself it is invisible. It can only be seen at the source or as it is reflected from something. Although the light of the sun fills the universe, outer space is in darkness until the light of the sun touches something from which it can be reflected. Jesus is the Light of the World, our Source. But in the world of spiritual darkness, His light can only be seen as it is reflected from us, as the moon reflects the light of the sun. May the Lord help us to be powerful reflections of His glory (John 1:1-4).

God often uses small matches to light great torches.

A steady drizzle was falling, making the darkness of the night heavy and thick. The headlights struggled to pierce the inky blackness on the curves of the mountain road. Finally, exhausted, I arrived at my destination about midnight. Although I had never been in this part of the country, I was too tired to look out into the murky night at my surroundings. I tumbled under the warm blankets and slept soundly.

When morning came, the warm sun shining across my face awakened me. Jumping up, I looked out of the window to see what the day was like. I was amazed as I gazed out over a beautiful mountain valley. Sun-bathed meadows sloped to the river. The forests stretched up, giving way to the distant snow-capped peaks. Oh, what a difference a little sunshine can make! I could never have imagined the beauty, the brightness, and the splendor of this place as I was strugging through the darkness of the night before.

Without Jesus Christ in our lives, we are in the darkness. No wonder the world is such a mess! No wonder there is so much hopelessness and despair! But oh, what a difference when Jesus comes into our lives! There is a total change.

Salvation brings dramatic transformation. The blind man Jesus healed said, *"I was blind, but now I see."* How many have given the same testimony when the light of God shines in their hearts! Not only initially does God's power produce this revolution, but also after we've become a Christian, His power gives us the option of responding to our situations by walking in His light or yielding to the darkness. John tells us to *"walk in the light as He is in the light"* (1 John 1:7).

In Luke 5, the disciples had been fishing all night, but caught nothing. Then Jesus came and told them to try again. This time, when they put down their nets, they were swamped with fish. When we toil long, and see no result, we are tempted to give up. Someone has said, "If at first you don't succeed, destroy all evidence that you ever tried!"

The Lord made the difference in the disciples' effort. When our efforts fail, hear the voice of the Lord— take courage, and try again!

Courage does not always roar. Sometimes it is the quiet voice at the end of the day, saying, "I will try again tomorrow."

The carpenters had just finished some renovation work in the office and had done a good job of sweeping up their mess. It was a cold day outside, -35° C, with a brisk wind. The house kept getting colder and colder. Why didn't the furnace cut in? A quick inspection showed me that the furnace fan was not working. On such a cold day, there was no choice but to make an emergency call to the furnace repairman forty kilometres away.

By the time he arrived, the house had become uncomfortably cool! With experienced step, the plumber headed down the stairs and looked into the furnace. Then he turned around, looked at the electric wall switch, and turned it on. Presto! We had lots of heat.

I stared in shock at the wall switch, and then understanding came. When the carpenters had been cleaning up, they had accidentally turned it off thinking it was a light switch. I hadn't thought of such a simple solution! Feeling extremely embarrassed and with a cramp in my pocketbook, I paid the $70 plumber's bill. He smiled and said something about fast, easy money.

While we search for complicated answers, God's solutions are often practical and right before us in His Word. We need only the patience and the courage to keep seeking His ways.

God spoke to Joshua in Joshua 1:2 and said,
"Moses my servant is dead; now therefore arise...."
God challenges us to rise up and keep on going!
There were great blessings in the past, but we need
to move on. The best is yet to come!

*You are truly successful when you can
look back in forgiveness, forward in hope,
and up with gratitude.*

It was the middle of the month of May. Just outside the kitchen door and overshadowing the front deck of the home where I was staying, stood a majestic spruce tree. Looking up into its branches, we had a bird's eye view of a robin's nest.

Discreetly blended and ingeniously secured among the entwined branches, this home had been built by a pair of red-breasted robins. When I got my first glimpse of the nest, the eggs had already hatched and the three siblings were rapidly growing in size, and developing feathers.

The moment Mother Robin landed in the tree near the nest, all three babies immediately opened their mouths wide and struggled to get the next juicy worm. That really intrigued me. Such expectancy! Such enormous appetites! Such rapid growth! Both parents were kept extremely busy searching for worms and bugs to stuff into those gaping mouths. Wouldn't it be wonderful if, as believers, we would have such anticipation, such appetite, and such spiritual growth?

Every now and then, perhaps when she needed a rest, Mother Robin would just sit on top of all of her noisy brood. Some mothers I know might appreciate the example and like to try the same method!

A few days later, it was apparent that these little birds were ready to leave the nest. One by one, the parents took them out on the limb. Their strength and confidence grew. In their first attempts to fly, they fluttered to the ground. Under the attentive eyes of their experienced parents, they fluttered around awhile and then finally mastered the art of take-off, soaring, and landing. Soon they too, would be strong, capable adults.

The Lord, who has watched over our spiritual growth, calls us out on a limb of faith. There are new horizons to reach. That calls for the stretching of our capacities. In daring to go forth, we find that God has given us everything we need to accomplish His plan.

Chapter Six

TRIUMPH OF TRUTH

Headlines tell of deceit, dishonesty, and debauchery. We are distressed by the ungodliness that pervades society. The tentacles of evil reach even to government officials. In despair we seek for righteousness. Soon, however, Christ will take His rightful place as King of kings. Truth shall overcome. John saw that day in Revelation 5:13:

> *"And every creature which is in heaven, and on the earth...heard I saying, Blessing, and honour, and glory, and power, be unto him that sitteth upon the throne, and unto the Lamb for ever and ever."*

In Isaiah, we read this promise: *"No weapon that is formed against thee shall prosper; and every tongue that shall rise against thee in judgment thou shalt condemn. This is the heritage of the servants of the LORD, and their righteousness is of me, saith the LORD."*

Truth will win. God will stand by His people. Let us keep our hearts pure; and let the Lord fight our battles.

Time is the best friend of the truth.

On the beach near Dieppe, France, I saw the stones that had been stained with the blood of hundreds of Canadians on August 17, 1942. Built into the cliffs above, were the crumbling hulks of huge enemy bunkers. In many places, as one travels through Europe, there are reminders of the fierce battles that have been fought: acres of military graveyards, cement bunkers looming out of the ground, and remnants of barbed wire barriers. War is so devastating.

Through their generations, men have built their kingdoms and their castles. At the cost of thousands of lives, some leaders have maintained their thrones for a few years, only to see them crumble into the rubble of time. How futile and vain is man's struggle for power.

Unless our lives are built on the Rock, Christ Jesus, we are vainly building air castles that will vanish in eternity. But when we are born again, with the assurance of eternal life, we are part of His everlasting kingdom that shall never be defeated.

I read this startling Scripture in Ezekiel 22:30, *"I sought for a man among them, that should build up the wall, and stand in the gap before me for the land, that I should not destroy it; but I found none"* (NASB). Terrible judgment was about to destroy the nation of Judah. The prophets had pleaded with the people to turn from their sin and rebuild the walls of righteousness... but to no avail.

The tragedy was, that in the entire nation, no one could be shaken out of apathy and unconcern for his soul, or for anyone else's. No one cared enough about righteousness and relationship with the Lord to try to make a difference. Who would the Lord find today? Would we be among them?

The role of the preacher is to comfort the afflicted and afflict the comfortable.

The wind was blowing cold, picking up the papers lying in the street. The glaring lights of downtown Copenhagen were endeavoring to entice people to every kind of human vice. There were wanderers and tourists meandering through the streets. Groups of men hovered around the doors of the porn shops; raucous laughter drifted out of the bars and disco halls. Among the crowds were staggering drunks and glassy-eyed drug addicts. Then there were the prostitutes. Young girls—and even middle-aged women—stood waiting. Their hard faces hid the broken hearts that were encrusted by pain and drug addiction.

My friends, pastors in a church in Copenhagen, are deeply involved in street evangelism. They had invited me to see their work and to take part in ministering in the street mission. It was a totally new adventure for me. Now, here I was walking the street with the pastor in the cold night, looking for hopeless hearts.

We stopped and chatted to frequent visitors of the mission. This type of work requires a great deal of patience, and searching for the harvest. It means pouring out the love and compassion of Christ and waiting for the moment when hearts at last surrender to the claims of Christ. It means picking through broken wrecks of humanity and looking for those who really want to be mended.

I listened with wonder to the testimonies of God's grace in many who have been rescued. They also had known utter ruin in their lives, but Jesus had touched them and given them a brand-new life. The power of drugs, alcohol, and immorality had been broken. They were free. They were whole again.

As I looked into the lonely eyes that surrounded me on the street, my heart was stirred. We must step out of our

111

comfort zones. We must show an aching world that Jesus is the answer. We must reach out in practical friendship evangelism, to touch the broken core of society. "Lord, give us a greater compassion, larger vision, and effective strategies to rescue souls from hell, to fill heaven," must be our cry.

In Genesis 3:1-6, we read of the temptation and fall of
Adam and Eve. The tactic of the enemy was to cause
Eve to focus on the one thing she did not have, causing
her to forget all she did have. This is often the root of our
temptations, our failure, and our sin. We first look,
then concentrate on what we do not have.
One secret of victory is to fix our vision on Christ
and what we do possess in Him.

*If you seek your Lord Jesus in all things, you will
truly find Him; but if you seek yourself, you will
find yourself; and that will be to your own
great loss. ——Thomas A. Kempis*

After experiencing extremely difficult driving conditions during the winter, I was very thankful to see the last of the icy roads. Having enjoyed one of my first beautiful, bright, warm, spring days, I was delighted to drive with renewed self-confidence. I backed slowly out of my friend's driveway, carefully watching some children playing in the street. Thud! I had hit the truck parked on the opposite side! There was very little damage done to my van, only a broken tail-light. There was no damage whatsoever to the other vehicle, but my pride suffered a serious blow!

After driving for months in such difficult conditions, passing at least forty or fifty major accidents with never a scratch, I had dented my van and my pride in the bright sunshine. How embarrassing!

Often in the dark and difficult moments of our lives, we call out to the Lord. Walking step by step in His grace, we hold tightly to His hand, seeking His protection and mercy to sustain us. Then when the problems disappear, we step out in our own strength and confidence, only to have a collision!

In 1 Samuel 30:6 we read: *"…David encouraged himself in the Lord his God."* In the time of trial when we are alone, like David, we can take God's Word and let it lift us above the darkness of our circumstances. People will often disappoint; trials may be difficult; nevertheless, if we will change our focus, letting the Lord's goodness permeate our thoughts, the joy and peace of God will fill our hearts.

Don't ever doubt in the darkness what God told you in the light.[5]

Laying down my book, I looked at the clock. It was about midnight and time to turn out the light. A movement on the wall caught my eye. It was a six-legged creature with a very long brown beetle-like body. *Cockroach!*

I'm not particularly squeamish and actually think mice are cute, but this was not a mouse. It was a slithery, sluggish bug. The sort that I thoroughly detest! In tropical countries they abound. I had seen lots of them before, but had always been able to call someone to kill them for me. This one was almost directly over my head. I could call no one to my rescue, as the whole household was sound asleep.

I climbed up on the table by the bed, book in hand, ready to swing a killing blow. In the shadows of the night-light, it looked three times larger than any I'd ever seen. I got down from the table, took another look from a respectable distance and then got up on the table again. After five or six exercises of this sort, I finally found the determination to give it a mighty whack.

I hate the sound of squishing bugs! When I lifted the book, I knew I had conquered the enemy. Often Satan comes at us in the dark moments of life. The temptations, fears, and circumstances seem larger than life. But as we rise with faith and stand our ground, we find Satan's power is no match for the Word of God.

Martin Luther is credited with saying,
"Everything that is done in the world is done by hope."
Some *hopes* go sour, but our eternal hope in Christ is sure.

Death is not terminal; it is transitional. It is not the end of the road, but a bend in the road. Death cannot kill what cannot die.[6]

I truly love my country of Canada, and often experience a surge of gratitude as I enjoy the natural beauty of this land. Having my young friend from Europe with me and seeing her expression of amazement, brought a new appreciation for the splendour of God's creation. As we looked together at those things that are so familiar to me, but which she was seeing for the first time, I realized again how wonderful Heaven is going to be. Although I had tried to explain what parts of Canada were like, ten minutes of actually being here was more effective than all my descriptions.

Jesus used the most eloquent and beautiful words in the human language to try to express to us what His Father's house was like. In the book of Revelation, John also tried to explain the wonders of Heaven, the majesty of God's throne and the beauty that awaits us there—but with all the descriptions, we still cannot fathom exactly what it will be. It surpasses human intellect and imagination. However, five minutes after we arrive, the questions will be answered and we will see Him face to face. With joy, He shall show us His Kingdom, His world.

Nothing is taking God by surprise! In the light of shocking, disheartening world events, our hearts can be at peace, knowing that He who made all things, knows the end from the beginning. The awesome finger of God radically humbled the great, proud, King Nebuchadnezzar. He declared in Daniel 4:35, *"...He does as he pleases with the powers of heaven and peoples of the earth. No one can hold back his hand or say to him: 'What have you done?'"* (NIV). Ultimately, God will have the last word.

The closer you get to God, the less you understand Him, but the more you believe Him.
—Corrie ten Boom

A stiff wind was blowing from the Mediterranean Sea as a friend and I walked down the street of Ajaccio, Corsica. This is an island province of France, situated between Italy and Spain. Ajaccio is also Napoleon Bonaparte's hometown. Everywhere, the street signs and hotels bear symbolic names and figures to bring remembrance to the name of the island's most famous hero. At the end of one street, a huge column has been erected with a staircase leading to a large statue of Napoleon on his horse. Inscribed on the column are his various victories and accomplishments. Just below his statue is written these words, "We have seen him climb with splendour, the first steps to heaven."

There were several things that were deeply etched on my mind, as I looked at this memorial to one of the world's most fascinating leaders. I was amazed again at the utter vanity of building earthly kingdoms. Those few short years of military victory, adoration, and power, have long since turned to dust. I noticed too, that conspicuously absent from the list of battles was any reference to Waterloo, that place of ignominious defeat.

It was a defeated and banished Napoleon whose own lips reputedly declared something like this: "Caesar, Charlemagne, and I have tried to construct our kingdoms by war and have failed. Jesus Christ built His kingdom by love and it has endured."

Looking at the cold stone statue, I was reminded of another King. He took more than the first steps to heaven: He went all the way! He went, not with a list of the victories of military might, but triumphant over all the powers of Satan. Jesus stands forever, the King of kings, the Lord of lords!

Chapter Seven

READY OR NOT

There are few certainties in life: death is one of them. Until the Lord returns, we all must pass by the grave. Preparation for this journey should be among our priorities. The Word of God gives us guidelines in Titus 2:12,13:

> *"Teaching us that, denying ungodliness and worldly lusts, we should live soberly, righteously, and godly, in this present world; Looking for that blessed hope, and the glorious appearing of the great God and our Savior Jesus Christ."*

The Gospel of John has been called the heart of the Bible, and John 3:16, the heart of God. Treasured by believers, this verse is probably the most memorized Scripture in the Bible. It shows us the great plan of salvation and offers us a living relationship with God through Jesus Christ, with the assurance of eternal life.

"For God so loved the world, that he gave his only begotten Son, that whosoever believeth in him should not perish, but have everlasting life" (John 3:16). Compared word by word, this verse reveals the *Greatest* Lover, degree of love, number of persons affected, act of love, gift, invitation, simplicity, person, deliverance, difference, certainty, and possession.

In spite of what God knows about us (and that is more than we know about ourselves), He loves us.

I had driven three hours through a steady drizzle to get to the town where I was to preach that day. A construction barricade was across the entrance road leading to the town some two kilometres away. I stopped. There was another entrance road farther on, but this one looked smooth enough, so I decided to give it a try.

Gingerly, I drove around the barricade and a few feet down the slight incline onto the new road. Once off the pavement, I made a horrible discovery. I was in gumbo! You have to experience it to understand it. It is dense Saskatchewan clay that, once waterlogged, has the consistency of thick grease and the properties of crazy-glue!

When I tried to back up, the van gently began to slide sideways toward a ten-foot ditch with water in it! It would be better to go ahead. For nearly a kilometre I ploughed forward. Suddenly, less than ten metres in front of me, I realized there was no road. The construction crew had dug a huge hole, preparing to lay a new roadbed. There was nothing to do but turn around. With much roaring and spinning and flying mud, I got the rig turned around. I started back toward the highway. The van was now loaded with the mud, which was sticking underneath. I was carrying two tons of muck!

When I came to the slight incline to go back up onto the highway, it was more than those mud-clogged wheels could take. The mud won! The wheels were so packed they could no longer turn. My only option was to flag someone down to call a tow truck.

Over an hour later I arrived at the church, feeling rather gooey with shoes caked three times their size in mud. The church began to sing a favourite hymn, "He brought me out of the miry clay." It could not have been more appropriate!

For many, sin and evil habits, *like that road,* look all right. They take a little step into it and they are trapped.

They try backing out, but they cannot. They try to turn around or dig themselves out with sheer will power. They only sink deeper. Their goodness, religion, money, or friends can't help them either. Drugs, alcohol, immorality, occultism, or religious ritualism bogs them down.

The Bible says in Romans 3:23, *"For all have sinned and come short of the glory of God."* We cannot set ourselves free or change our own hearts. Only Jesus can break sin's deadly grip, wash the mud from our hearts, save our souls, and set us free.

Psalmist David declared in Psalm 40:2: *"He brought me up also out of an horrible pit, out of the miry clay and set my feet upon a rock...."*

As a young man, David lived on the edge. His life was in constant jeopardy because of the insane jealousy of King Saul. More than once he narrowly escaped death at the hand of his enemy. It led him to pray in Psalm 31:15: *"My times are in thy hand: deliver me from the hand of mine enemies, and from them that persecute me."* We all need to be reminded, "Our times are in God's hands." Let us live wisely today, for we do not know if we will be here tomorrow.

At age twenty, we worry about what others think of us. At forty, we don't care what they think of us. At sixty, we discover they haven't been thinking of us at all.

It was about 35° C, with high humidity. I was assured that the most economical, practical way to travel between two points through the crowded Taiwanese streets was by scooter. Helmets were rarely worn, because of the heat. The missionary's wife and I were presently one with hundreds of others working our way through the dusty, crowded streets. It didn't take me long to get the hang of *hanging on*. The heavy traffic, with cars and trucks zooming by, made me feel somewhat apprehensive.

Then I saw it happen right in front of my eyes. A car ran into the back of a woman's scooter beside us. No one was hurt, although there were some flying sparks from all parties concerned. Sometime later, I saw a much more serious accident that had happened before we passed the scene.

Bouncing along amidst thousands of others riding down the street, I began to relax. As a part of this crowd, I actually felt that nothing would happen to me—a little invincible perhaps.

It was later, when I looked out from the safety of my room at the masses of scooters, that I realized how quickly we could be desensitized to danger. Jesus often used words like *watch, be alert, and be ready*. It is easy for us to become so involved with the busyness of the crowd (the going, and the doing) that we forget the shortness of life and the imminent return of Christ.

The Scripture tells us in Psalm 34:7: *"The angel of the LORD encampeth round about them that fear him, and delivereth them."* How many times in a day or, in some of my adventures, in an hour, has the unseen angel of the Lord been sent to protect or direct? Perhaps frustrating delays and chance encounters have been orchestrated by angels watching out for us!

God will never let anything come your way that you and He cannot handle.

The homemade turkey soup was fabulous. I was scooping it up with delight. Then I felt a bone. It passed over my tongue but before I could catch it, it started down my throat. I swallowed hard. It passed the windpipe and then stopped. It instantly created a real pain in the neck!

Realizing that the turkey bone was stuck and not knowing if its position was a serious hazard to the health; we decided to go to Emergency. Although I could breathe easily, I didn't know what would happen if it moved. During the thirty-minute drive to the hospital, I did some serious thinking about Heaven, about dying, and about how much I was enjoying this life. I had the morbid vision of newspaper headlines, "Evangelist Chokes to Death on Turkey Bone." It was not exactly the way or time I wanted to exit this life.

Four hours later, after I was admitted in preparation for medical intervention, the bone suddenly loosened and went down. What a relief! I was overjoyed! Honestly, I almost kissed the doctor!

Life is so uncertain. At any given time, we are only one heartbeat from death; we are only one breath from eternity. The Bible says in James 4:4, "*Whereas ye know not what shall be on the morrow. For what is your life? It is even a vapour, that appeareth for a little time, and then vanisheth away.*"

What peace to have the assurance of eternal life, to know that death is not the end, but a beginning! Through faith in Jesus Christ we have eternal hope, a home prepared where we shall be forever with the Lord.

Daily we watch the devastation of war reported on our television newscasts. It seems there are new wars starting every day! It is unbelievable to see the incredible human suffering and to observe history repeating itself, more savagely than ever. Whoever said that civilization is improving, has only to look at five minutes of news to know that there is nothing new under the sun. *The heart of man is deceitful and desperately wicked* (Jeremiah 17:9).

That's the bad news. The good news is what Jesus said in Luke 21:28: *"When these things begin to take place, stand up and lift up your heads, because your redemption is drawing near"* (NIV).

God whispers to us in our pleasures,
speaks in our conscience, but shouts in our pain.
It is His megaphone to rouse a deaf world.
——C.S. Lewis

At 8:15 on the morning of August 6, 1945, the world's first atomic bomb was dropped on Hiroshima. Almost the entire city was devastated in that single moment. Thousands of people were instantly killed. Some literally evaporated so quickly in the tremendous heat, their shadows were all that remained. During the following year, the toll reached over 340,000 who had died as a direct result of this horror.

Three types of energy compounded the damage done by the atomic bomb: heat rays, which reached thousands of degrees at hypocentre; blast pressure, which reached several tons of pressure per square inch, crushing buildings and people; and radiation, which produced long-lasting, even unknown damage.

One afternoon, while ministering in Japan, we went to the city of Hiroshima. In the centre of the new city there is a memorial museum of this tragedy. I stood transfixed with horror in front of one of the exhibits. The stone steps had once been the entrance to a large bank. A person had been sitting on the step, probably waiting for the bank to open. In a moment, on that fateful morning, the powerful flash of light and fire seared the stones white. But the stones where the person had been sitting had been shielded in that brief millisecond, from the first light. They were now clearly marked by the shadow of the body that had vaporized.

Looking at the pictures, the charred clothing, the melted glass, and twisted steel, I could not help but think of the prophecies that describe what will happen on the earth at the end of time. Long before nuclear energy was even dreamt of, its devastating effects were perfectly described by the Old Testament prophet in Zechariah 14:12.

In light of present world events, we need to be often reminded of what is written in 2 Peter 3:10,11:

But the day of the Lord will come like a thief. The heavens will disappear with a roar; the elements will be destroyed by fire, and the earth and everything in it will be laid bare. Since everything will be destroyed in this way, what kind of people ought you to be? You ought to live holy and godly lives as you look forward to the day of God and speed its coming (NIV).

Moses, who wrote Psalm 90:12, prayed that the Lord would *"Teach us to number our days, that we may apply our hearts unto wisdom."* It is a wise person indeed that recognizes the preciousness of life and time. Let us not waste a minute of either.

No one on his deathbed has said, "I wish I had spent more time at work."

The airport was bustling with activity as I stood in line at the check-in counter, but I had nothing to hurry about. All of the plans had been carefully made months before. I casually handed my ticket to the agent. A strange expression crossed her face. She exclaimed, "But this ticket is dated for a flight yesterday!"

Yesterday! I nearly fainted! Because of my mistake in dates and weekdays, I had missed an important flight by a whole day! I was shocked, horrified, but mostly embarrassed! A frequent international traveller who boasted about being well organized, I had overlooked one of the most important aspects of the trip... the date! The embarrassment of the moment and the awful sense of having been left behind soon passed as new flight plans were arranged.

The Bible makes it clear that everyone will someday stand before the Judgment Throne of Christ. There shall be those clutching their self-made tickets: church membership, water baptism, and good works.... What unspeakable horror to hear Christ say, *"I'm sorry, I never knew you."* It's not by our works, but by the Blood of Jesus Christ alone that we have access to eternal life (Matthew 25:41; Romans 6:23; Titus. 3:5).

Believers, let us also take warning. There shall be a day when we shall have our last opportunities to pray, to give, to go. Don't miss it because of selfishness, materialism, carelessness, or the love of pleasure. Check the rules for the ticket! Keep close to Jesus and His Word. Don't be too late.

The return of Christ is certain. We do not know when, but it will happen. Jesus warned the disciples in Luke 12:40: *"Be ye therefore ready also: for the Son of man cometh at an hour when ye think not."*

Man says, "Time is passing."
Time says, "Man is passing."

Dozing, while balancing with baggage on bony airport benches, demands skill. After twenty-eight hours of airplane travel, I was losing the skill. The transatlantic flight had arrived in Frankfurt nearly two hours late, causing me to miss my connection for Brussels. I had drowsily waited three hours for the next flight.

I jerked to full consciousness. They should have called us to board long ago. I jumped to the counter. With disinterest, the ticket agent informed me that my plane was already boarding at the other end of the airport!

I had not a second to lose! Galloping like a camel with a slipped-to-the-side-hump, my fifteen-kilo tote bag thumping against me with every step, I raced up stairs, down stairs, asked here, then ran there. I arrived at the gate, gasping for air. With pleading eyes and desperate voice, I asked if I could still make it to the plane. The agent looked solemn as she said, "I doubt it, but we'll try."

If I didn't make this connection, I would have to wait several hours. I was already exhausted. If only I had paid attention to the billboard. If only I had listened to the announcements! How could I possibly have slept through such important information! The long seconds ticked by as I panted, leaning against the counter. To be so close and yet so far—why had I allowed myself to fall asleep at such a critical time?

The agent returned. With a smile, she said, *"You made it!"* I ran up the ramp and thumped into my airplane seat. The door closed behind me; the plane started to move.

It is one thing to nearly miss a plane—far more serious to think of eternal matters. Jesus told us to ever be watching and waiting, ready to stand before His presence.

Don't be like the foolish virgins that Jesus told us about in Matthew 25:5,6:

The bridegroom was a long time in coming, and they all became drowsy and fell asleep. At midnight the cry rang out: 'Here's the bridegroom! Come out to meet him!' (NIV).

Jesus admonishes us to be ready. Are you ready to meet Him?

One of the most comforting passages in the Word of God is found in John 14:1-3, *"Let not your heart be troubled: ye believe in God, believe also in me. In my Father's house are many mansions: if it were not so, I would have told you. I go to prepare a place for you. And if I go and prepare a place for you, I will come again, and receive you unto myself; that where I am, there ye may be also."*

Once, while riding on a train in the mountains, we wound our way tortuously through the treacherous canyons in the blackness of the storm. Presently, we entered a dark tunnel. When we came through the other side, we burst into a broad valley full of sunlight.

For those who have made peace with God, I suppose death shall be something like that—out of pain into gain; out of earth into glory; out of clay vessels into eternal tabernacles; out of mortality into immortality; out of time into eternity, forever in the presence of Jesus.

Never complain about getting old.
Many do not have that privilege.

The health of an elderly friend who had consistently lived his faith in Christ, was failing quickly. It became apparent that he would not recover. As family and friends gathered to offer prayer and support, the inevitable was happening. That which every human being must one day experience, was unfolding. With every tick of the clock, life was ebbing away. Waiting, we counted heartbeats to eternity, yet dreading loss and parting pain. Strange it is, this paradox of time speeding by, yet standing still.

In a moment the waiting was over; the river was crossed; the soul departed. Sad but amazing—this living, breathing body was left like a discarded coat, crumpled and faded. The body that had served its master well was empty—just a shell of clay. The real person was no longer there!

In spite of loss, there is overwhelming hope, and unexplainable peace. Personal faith in the Lord Jesus and His Word assures the reality of the eternal soul, and hope beyond death. Gazing at the lifeless body powerfully reminded me that I too shall one day leave this temporal house of clay for my eternal home with Christ.

Except the Lord returns soon, we shall all pass that valley and cross that river. Like an avalanche that takes everything in its path, unstoppable is this fact of death. Each breath and heartbeat brings it nearer. Material possessions, proud accomplishments, and loud accolades will mean little then.

What will our friends and acquaintances say of us when we are gone? What will God say of us? What do we wish they would say? We may still have time to prepare our eulogy.

Conclusion

These personal reflections are meant to bring fresh inspiration and courage to you. The certainty of the Lord's sovereign control on the world scene assures us He can intervene in answer to our prayers. He demands the allegiance of our will. What less can we give when He has done so much for us?

We cannot change our circumstances; however, we do have power to choose our attitudes and responses. Our choices have eternal consequences. Planned with a purpose, we must not be distracted from the highest destiny God has designed for us. As the flowers that grow ever upward, reaching for the sun, we should desire to dwell in His light.

The dynamic of faith has been placed within the heart of those who surrender to Christ. The assurance and peace of His presence defies the darkness; with eagles' wings, we soar in hope.

We could compare humanity's ambitions to an intense game of chess. Men have played their strategies against

God. They have tried their best to greedily gain the gratification of their pride. In the final moment of time, however, God shall win the game and Truth shall triumph.

The choice is put to you and me. We shall stand before the Judge of all the earth. John the Beloved gives this word of admonition in I John 2:28: *"And now, little children, abide in him; that, when he shall appear, we may have confidence, and not be ashamed before him at his coming."* In His presence, at journey's end, we shall forever be *above the storm.*

The Gift of Salvation

If you have never given your life to Christ, it is my hope that you will surrender to Him today. According to Romans 3:23: *"For all have sinned, and come short of the glory of God."*

The Bible tells us that peace with God is received by turning to Him from our sins. In Romans 10:9,10, we read:

That if thou shalt confess with thy mouth the Lord Jesus, and shalt believe in thine heart that God hath raised him from the dead, thou shalt be saved. For with the heart man believeth unto righteousness; and with the mouth confession is made unto salvation.

In verse 13 it is written: *"For whosoever shall call upon the name of the Lord shall be saved."* You can receive His life now by repentance and faith. Pray this simple prayer.

"Lord, I know I have sinned. I believe You are the Son of God and that You died on the cross to forgive my sins. I believe You have risen from the dead with power to give me a transformed life. Please forgive me, change my heart and set me free. I surrender the control of my will to You. Help me to follow You. In Jesus' Name. Amen."

Read the Bible and pray every day. Find others who love Jesus, who can help you to follow Him. With your hand in the hand of Jesus, you will finish your journey with joy.

Notes

---

[1] T. F. Tenney, *The Main Thing...is to Keep the Main Thing the Main Thing* (Hazelwood: Word Aflame Press, 1993) 188

[2] Tenney, p. 110

[3] Tenney, p. 26

[4] Tenney, p. 108

[5] Tenney, p. 115

[6] Tenney, pp. 42, 36

I have attempted to give credit where credit is due. If something is not properly credited, this was not intentional. Some sources could not be identified.

Bibliography

Gibbon, Edward. *The Rise and Fall of the Roman Empire.* Ed. Dero A. Saunders. U.S.A.: Penguin Press, 1983.

Maxwell, John. *The Winning Attitude.* San Bernardino: Here's Life Publishers, Incorporated, 1991.

Tenny, T. F. *The Main Thing...is to Keep the Main Thing the Main Thing.* Hazelwood: Word Aflame Press, 1993.

Please visit Anita's Web site,
www.inspirationministries.net
for a complete catalogue of her
music, videos,
and other ministry information.

Inspiration Ministries Music

by Anita Pearce

For song lists, please visit www.inspirationministries.net

Grace (CD)
Cassette: $14.00
CD: $20.00

Mercy (CD)
Cassette: $14.00
CD: $20.00

To order, send cheque or money order, including $6.00 shipping,
to:
Inspiration Ministries
Box 44
Margo, SK
Canada S0A 2M0
OR you can order online. All prices are in Canadian funds.